The Untrapped Butterfly

Kay Underdown

The Untrapped Butterfly
reflections on life
and photo memories
ISBN 978-1-912899-10-4 paperback
ISBN 978-1-912899-11-1 ebook

Author Kay Underdown

Published Winter 2023

Waves and Pebbles Publishing

For You

a book to inspire creativity

and your own life story project

with the freedom to write or draw

your own ideas, plans,

thoughts and memories

on the pages

K

A Snapshot Intro

This book is the result of a clearing process as I move into a new phase of my life. It captures personal memories in a way that can be shared verbally with others and each time a different story may emerge.

In Autumn 2015, I felt the need to visit Brighton when facing my last course of cancer treatment.

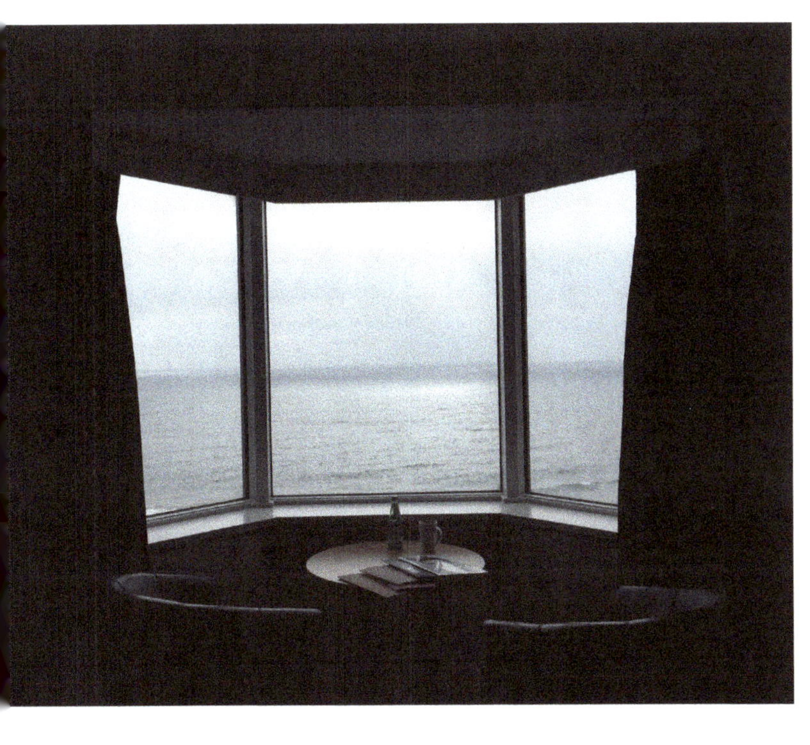

One day the sky will fall
the unimaginable will happen

Don't wait for that day

Venture into a new tomorrow
with a fresh zest for life

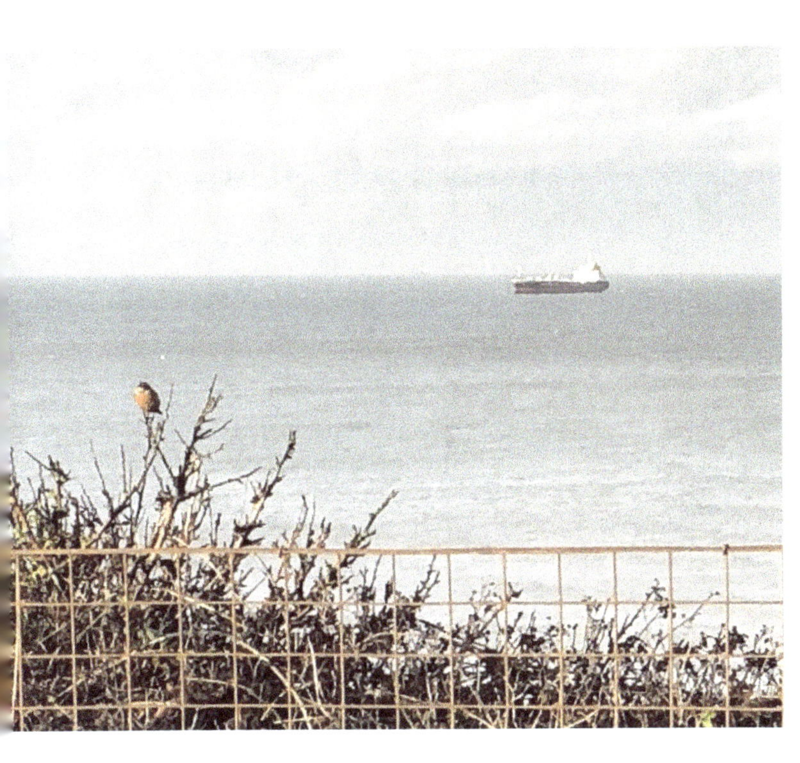

If ever there was a time to embrace
all that has been so wonderful
in your life
it is now

So often, it is the negative stuff
that manages to draw our attention
let go, let go
and feel the weight slide
off your shoulders
as it melts away

Where there is hope, there is forever
a means of turning things around
and the lighter the load,
the way becomes clearer

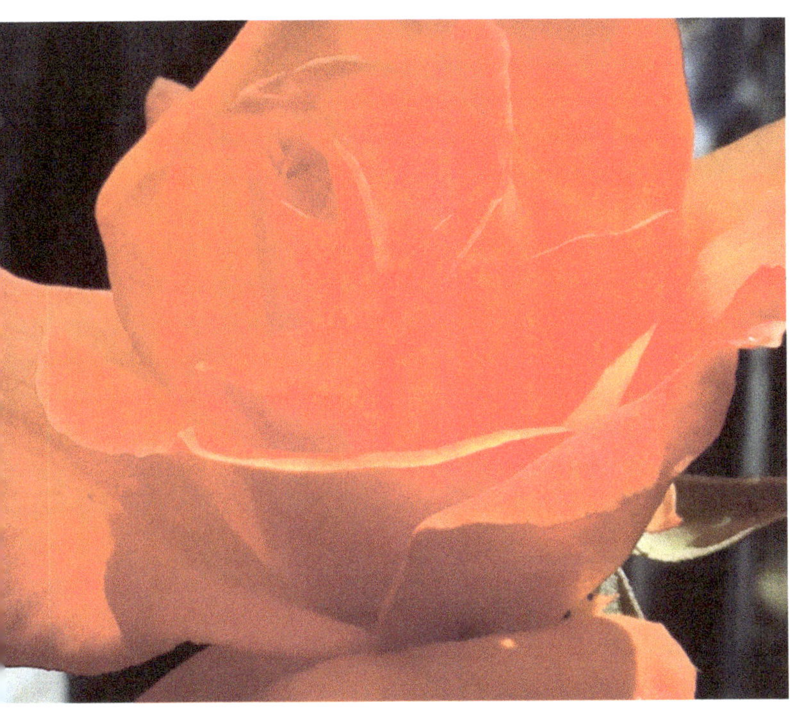

In the darkness is to be found
peace, stillness
most best is the softness of the
moonlight
that wipes away all the doubt
and allows the moment to shine

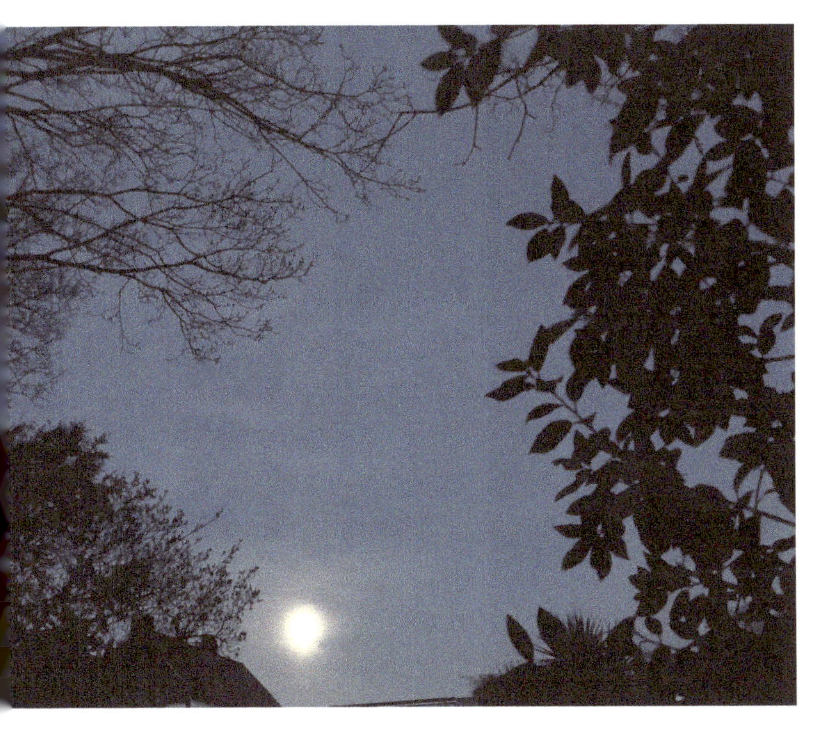

Whatever dreams you may have
let them sway
like the trees in the wind
going with the flow
with good roots, know that they're OK

Whatever thoughts you may have
they're precious
like jewels sprinkled on a moonlit pond
with respect, know that they're secure

Whatever love you may have
'tis a gift
like nothing else in the world
with love, know that you love

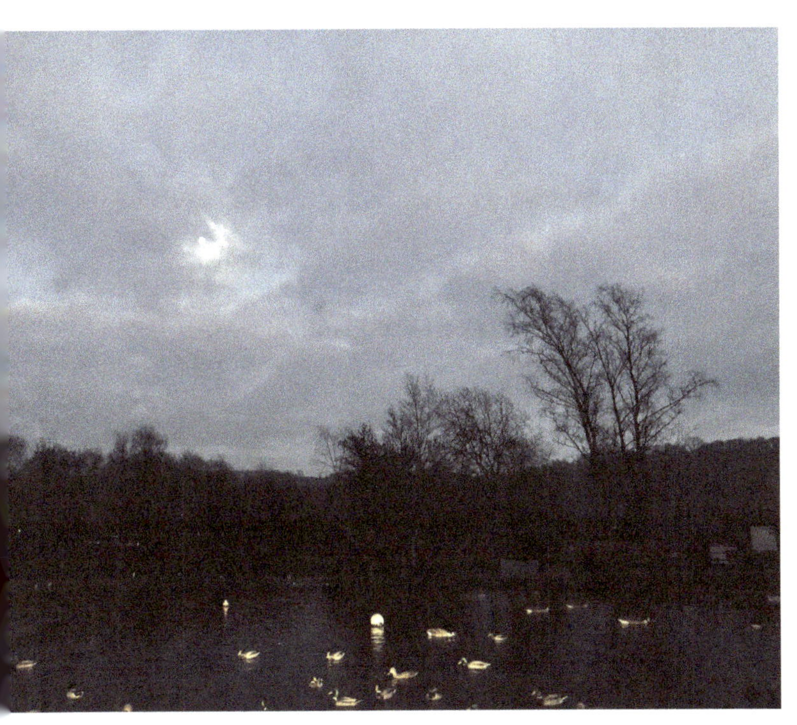

As I sit here under the leaves
I wonder what new adventure awaits me

Wondering allows the moments to pass
while dwelling on that which brings
a sense of unknowingness,
indecision and hopelessness.

Yet, if I so choose, wondering leads to the
magic of dreams not yet imagined that bring
a sense of excitement, possibility,
and a world awaiting our hidden talents
to emerge and spread their wings

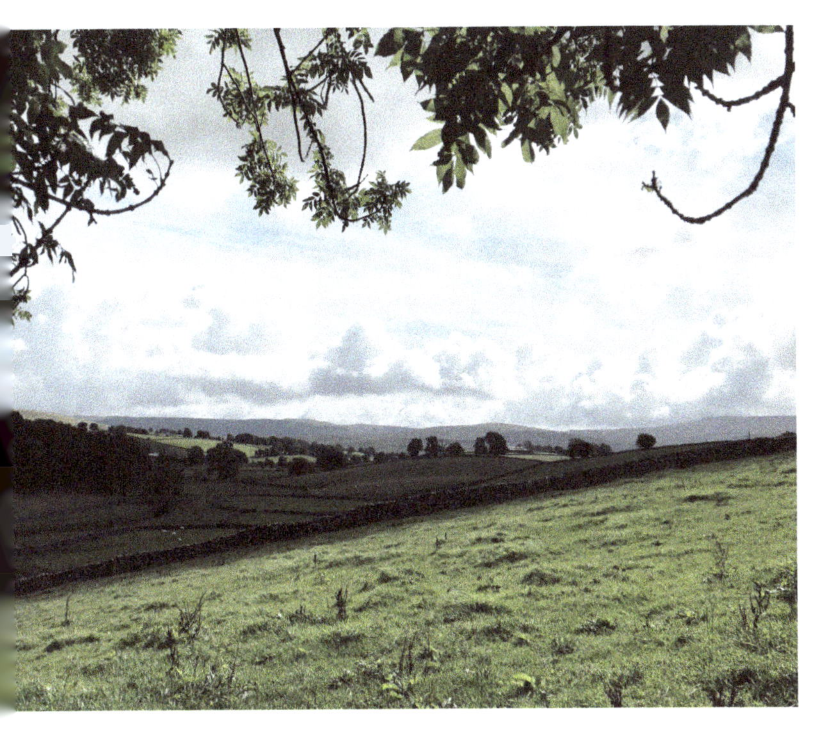

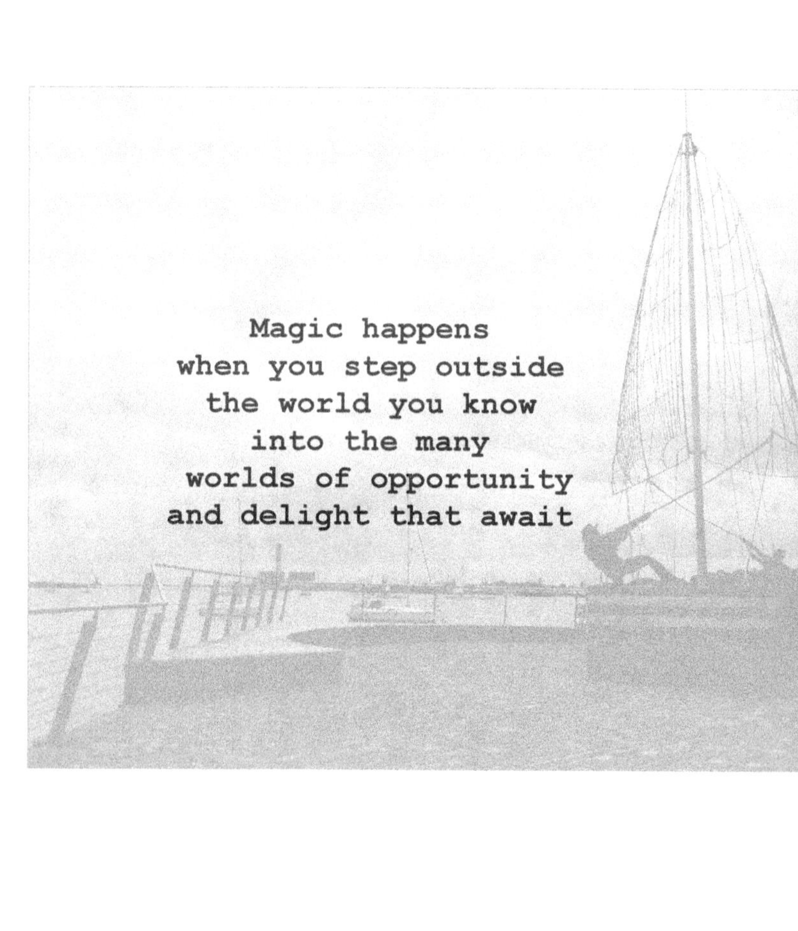

Magic happens
when you step outside
the world you know
into the many
worlds of opportunity
and delight that await

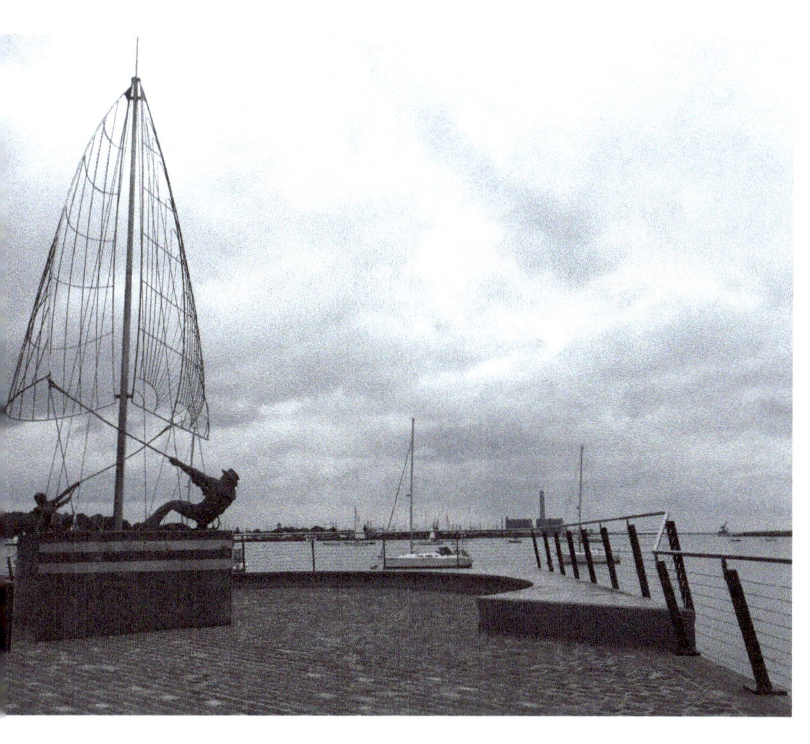

If there was one thing
that you never would do
but it sticks forever in your world
consider that you could just choose
to do it

If not, let it fade away
and bring new life into tomorrow

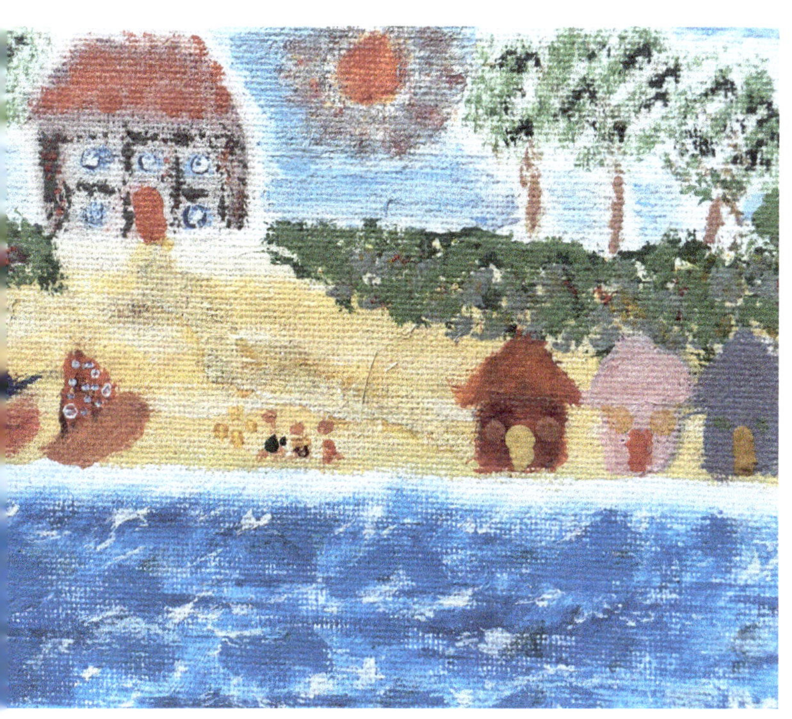

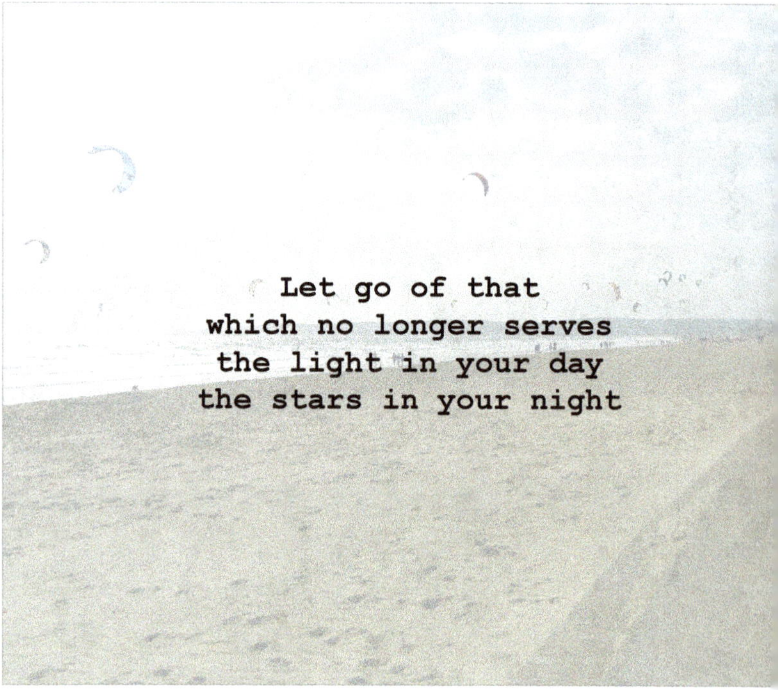

Let go of that
which no longer serves
the light in your day
the stars in your night

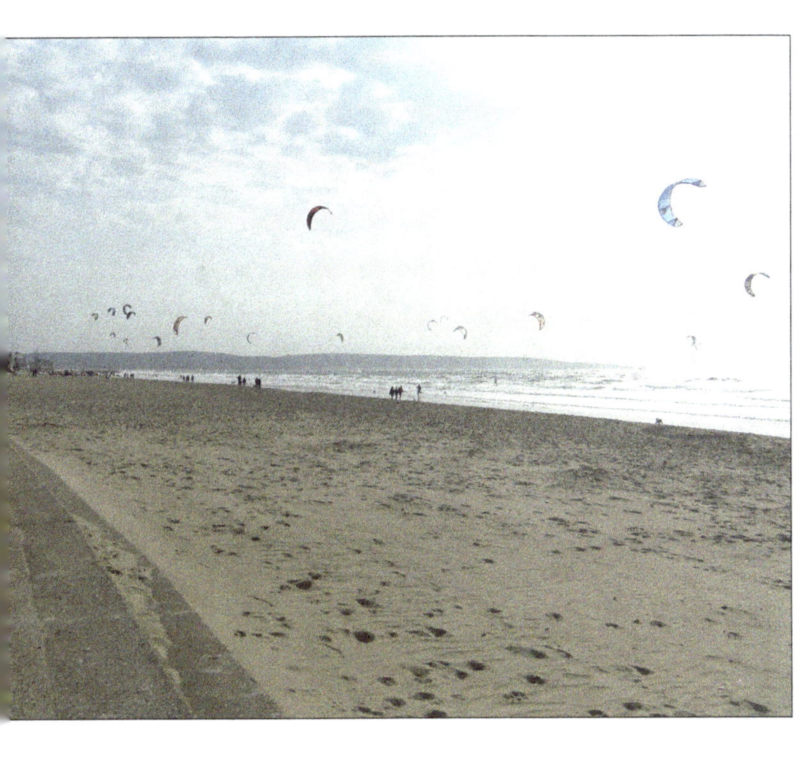

The Untrapped Butterfly

I am no longer trapped
there is no spider's web
it is an illusion

Let the light shine in
allow the darkness to transform
into a magical snowflake

As it melts away
in the soft warm hug of the sun
brightness and sparkle lead the way

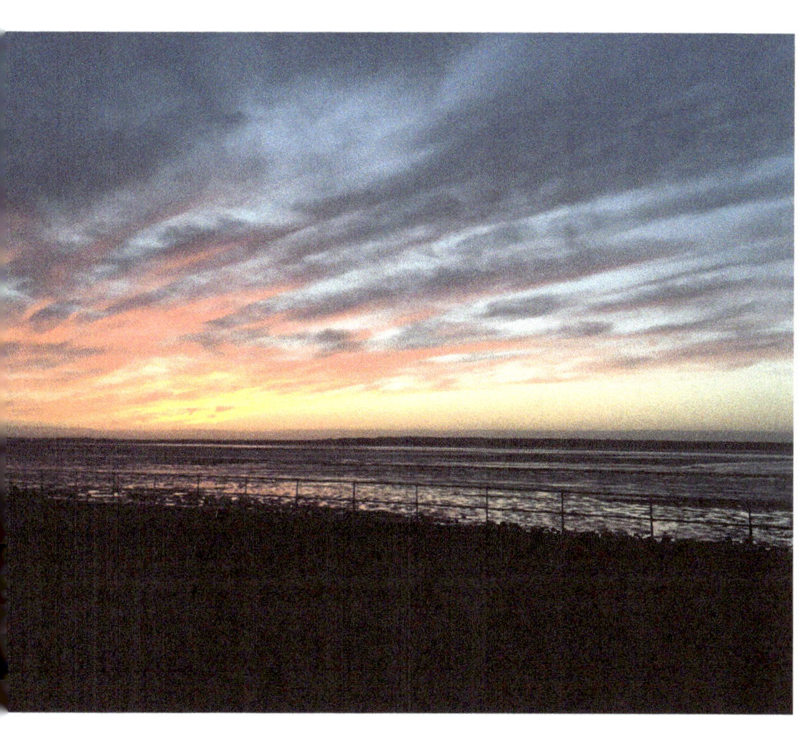

Calmness is in the air
I look out onto the dilapidated magnolias
no longer the vibrant hit of
white floral beauty
the flowers are wilting
tinged with an aura of sandy brown

Yet I have come to learn
that there is such beauty to be found
in the passing of time
when age takes its toll
whether that is in days, weeks,
months or years

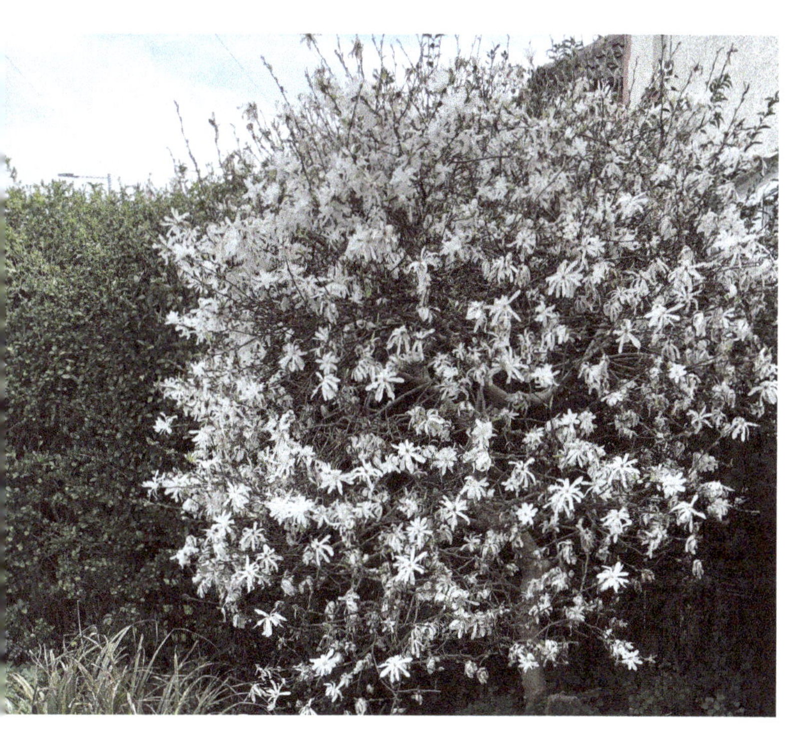

Savour each and every day
each and every hour
every minute

Especially those fleeting moments,
those that bring a sense of joy,
complete awe and belonging

In a world that never ceases
to amaze and surprise
in the most natural ways

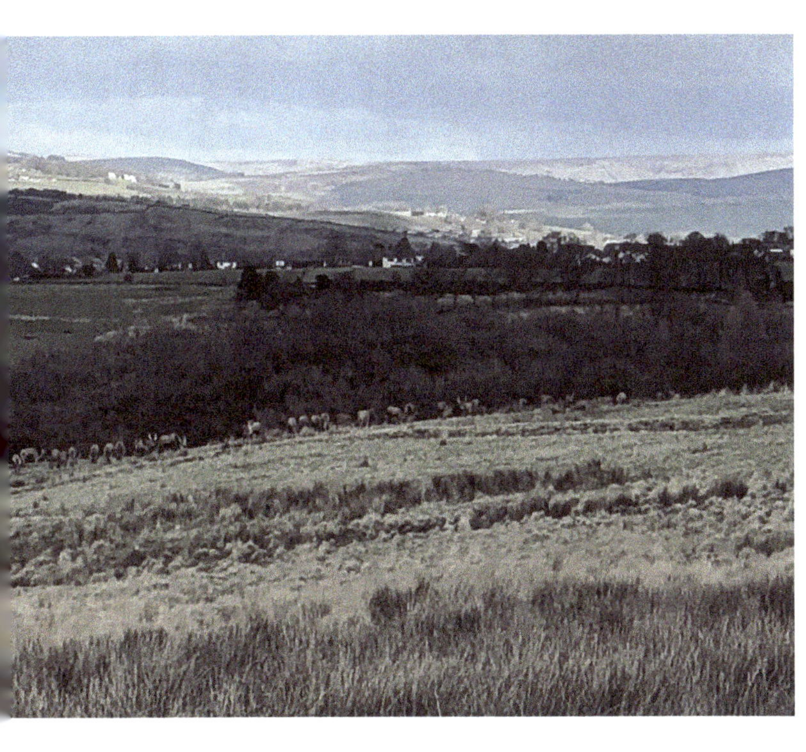

I close my eyes
feel the warmth of the radiating sun
hear the ebb and flow of the traffic

I am surrounded by song-singing tweets
as I soak up
the flourishing flowers and foliage

An array of music is growing deep within

I am re-immersed into the wondrous
oh so beautiful sea

It feels like heaven

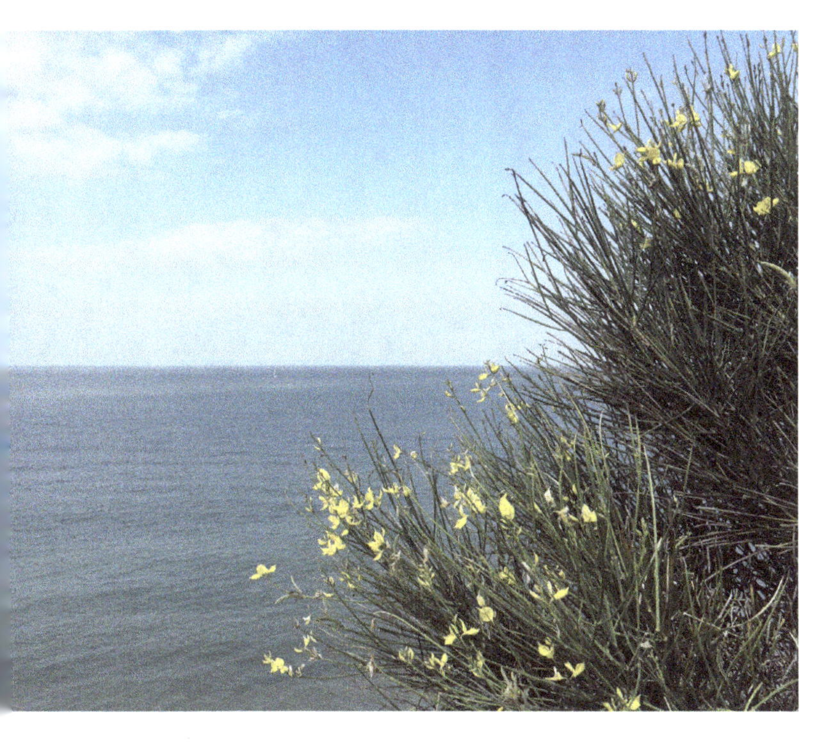

As I was born
nearby the waves were throbbing
the saltiness was in the air
and I was destined
to be a sea lover

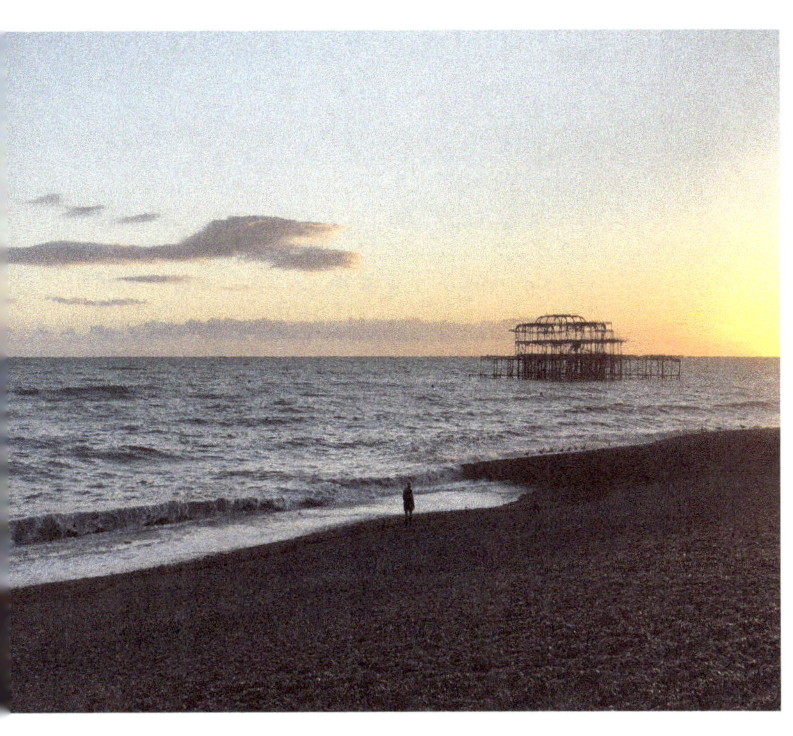

Captured within this little book is a random selection of writing extracted whilst sifting through past notebooks and scraps of paper. The photos are my own, chosen for their separate memories and meaning. In my recently published book, *Ripples*, that brought together 10 personal poems with photos, I decided to include endnotes. This time I have taken a more minimalistic approach.

You may wish to take a look at my book *Writing Back to Happiness, How to write the little stories in life*, written in collaboration with four lovely ladies when I lived on the Isle of Thanet. It includes writing prompts and life coaching exercises, and explains my own approach of Life Story Writing along with many examples. My first book, *Life Happens Live Happy*, was based around my experience of being diagnosed with a life-threatening form of leukaemia and written in the hope of inspiring others to use creativity and a positive approach to life to help overcome life challenges - more information on my blog www.wavesandpebbles.blog.

Whilst I have taken care in creating this book, if any errors slip in I apologise. However, I also believe that we don't have to aim for perfection and anything unintended becomes a part of the story. Kay

www.ingramcontent.com/pod-product-compliance
Lightning Source LLC
Chambersburg PA
CBHW061653050726
47598CB00004B/1562